JEWISH AND GNOSTIC MAN

Gilles Quispel
The Birth of the Child
Some Gnostic and Jewish Aspects

Gershom Scholem
Three Types of Jewish Piety

Spring Publications, Inc.
Dallas, Texas

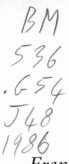
Eranos Lectures 3

Published by Spring Publications, Inc.; P.O. Box 222069; Dallas, Texas 75222
Printed in the United States of America

Cover design and production by Maribeth Lipscomb and Patricia Mora

International Distributors
Spring; Postfach; 8800 Thalwil; Switzerland
Japan Spring Sha, Inc.; 1–2–4, Nishisakaidani-Cho; Ohharano, Nishikyo-Ku; Kyoto, 610–11, Japan
Element Books Ltd; Longmead; Shaftesbury Dorset SP7 8PL; England

Library of Congress Cataloging-in-Publication Data
Main entry under title:

Jewish and Gnostic man.
   (Eranos lectures, ISSN 0743–586X ; 3)
   Contents: The birth of the child / G. Quispel.—Three
types of Jewish piety / G. Scholem.
    1. Judaism—Relations—Gnosticism. 2. Gnosticism—
Relations—Judaism. 3. Spiritual life—Judaism.
4. Jewish way of life. I. Quispel, Gilles, 1916–   The birth
of the child. II. Scholem, Gershom Gerhard, 1897–
Three types of Jewish piety. III. Series.
BM536.G54J48 1986   296.3'8   85–26137
ISBN 0–88214–403–0

Eranos Lectures series: ISSN 0743–586X

Acknowledgments
"Three Types of Jewish Piety" was a lecture presented originally at the 1969
Eranos Conference in Ascona, Switzerland, and appeared in the *Eranos Yearbook* 38—1969 (Ascona: Eranos Foundation, 1972), pp. 331–48. It is published
here with the kind permissions of the heirs of Gershom Scholem and the Eranos
Foundation. "The Birth of the Child" was a lecture presented originally at the
1971 Eranos Conference in Ascona, Switzerland, and appeared as translated by
Ruth Horine in the *Eranos Yearbook* 40—1971 (Ascona: Eranos Foundation,
1973), pp. 285–309. It is published here with the kind permissions of the author
and the Eranos Foundation.

Gilles Quispel

The Birth of the Child
Some Gnostic and Jewish Aspects

In his book *Eclipse of God* the Jewish philosopher Martin Buber described the psychologist C. G. Jung as a Gnostic. The statement was not intended as a compliment, because, according to Buber, Gnosticism and not atheism is the true enemy and opponent of faith in the Jewish or Christian sense of the word. His attitude was based on the view that Judaism and Gnosticism never had anything in common and therefore were irreconcilable antagonists even during the first centuries of the Christian era. The same view is held by Hans Jonas, who did not even mention Judaism as the root and background of Gnosticism in his epoch-making book entitled *Gnosis und spätantiker Geist*. Any views to the contrary were considered by him to represent the futile vanity of certain Jewish scholars on the one hand and that of decadent psychological circles on the other.[1] According to him, Gnosticism cannot possibly be derived from Judaism, and wherever it uses Jewish concepts, as that of a creator of the universe or demiurge, it distorts them. Furthermore, he claimed that the Jewish material that had been incorporated by Gnosticism had been given a purely negative interpretation.

As long as research into Gnosis confines itself to the pheno-

---

[1] G. Quispel, Gnosticism and the New Testament, in *The Bible in modern scholarship*, ed. by J.Ph. Hyatt, Nashville, 1965, 252-271; idem, The Origins of the Gnostic Demiurge, in *Kyriakon. Festschrift Johannes Quasten*, ed. by P. Granfield and J. A. Jungmann, Münster, 1970, 271-276.

menological method, it can hardly come up with another evaluation. For, in looking at the essence of the Gnostic religion, it becomes obvious that there is a fundamental difference between the Jewish and the Gnostic approach. Gnosis is based on the idea that there is something in man, his unconscious spirit, which is related to the ground of being. In order to restore the wholeness it has lost, the deity has an interest in redeeming this spiritual principle in man. Phenomenologically speaking, this concept has nothing in common with the Jews' reality affirming approach to creation.

What may seem phenomenologically impossible, may, however, prove to be quite possible in historical terms. The Gnostic records found near Nag Hammadi in Egypt seem to show that the influence of Judaism on Gnosticism was considerable.

This became evident as soon as the first document of the discovery at Nag Hammadi, the Valentinian *Gospel of Truth*, was published in 1956. This meditation on Christ and the Self includes extensive commentaries on Christ as the proper name of God, i.e., as revealing His essence. *Kurion onoma* as such is, of course, a *terminus technicus* used in Stoic philosophy. However, it was apparently taken over by the Jews to hint at the hidden, secret unmentionable name of God. *Shem hammephorash* is identical with *shem a hmmejuhhad* (proper name) in Jewish source material, and in esoteric Judaism this name was of great significance. There is therefore no doubt that the Valentinian author of the *Gospel of Truth* took over and incorporated a Jewish concept.

In its present form, the *Gospel according to Thomas*, a collection of *Logia* also found at Nag Hammadi, seems to indicate that its redactor was a Gnostic, at least on the basis of present interpretations. The words attributed to Jesus in this Gospel reveal an independent tradition and were transmitted by Jewish Christian circles. Evidence to this effect is provided by the fact that the Lord's brother James, the Pope of Jewish Christianity, appears in this document as Jesus' legitimate heir and the ruler of the entire Church. Jewish Christianity was, however, a Jewish sect, which, it would seem, influenced Gnosticism in this respect.

Furthermore, it became increasingly obvious that the figure of Sophia, which played a central role in many Gnostic systems as a world spirit in exile and as a cosmogonic power, must be traced back to the Jewish *Hokhma* of the Old Testament and to Jewish schools of Wisdom.

It is perfectly possible that, as tradition has it, the transition from the Jewish to the Gnostic concept of wisdom took place in the school of Simon Magus of Samaria. In the Palestinian Targum as well as in Samaritan liturgy, "beginning" was the equivalent of "wisdom". "In the beginning God created the heaven and the earth" eventually became "in his wisdom God created the heaven and the earth". This is the premise for Simon's view, according to which Helena, or Sophia, emerged from God in order to create the rulers of the world, who then, however, overwhelmed and imprisoned her.

It should be recalled that the Samaritans were a heterodox Jewish group, and the question concerning the relationship between Gnosis and Judaism cannot be answered as long as we identify present-day Rabbinical Judaism with the Judaism of those days. At that time, Palestine harboured not only Pharisees, but also Essenes, Baptists, Samaritans, Wisdom teachers, Jewish Christians, as well as a host of heretics of all kinds. As Gershom Scholem demonstrated, there were even a number of strict Pharisees in Palestine who handed down esoteric traditions known to the Gnostics and which later gave rise to a truly Jewish form of Gnosis, the *Kabbalah*.

Until recently it seemed impossible to find convincing evidence to show that the classic Gnosis of antiquity developed or was able to develop out of Judaism.

The Cologne *Mani Codex* seems to be of particular importance in this connection, because it shows how Gnosis evolved out of Judaism, or Jewish Christianity, as a result of a dialectical process.[1]

On the one hand there is no doubt that the Manichaean myth

---

[1] A. Henrichs und L. Koenen, Ein griechischer Mani-Codex, *Zeitschrift für Papyrologie und Epigraphik*, 5, 1970, 97-216.

described a Gnostic experience, namely the encounter with the
Self. The Codex tells how "the Twin" revealed himself to Mani at
the age of 25:

> I recognized him
> and understood that he was my Self,
> from whom I had been separated.[1]

On the other hand we now have proof that from the age of
four to twenty-five, i.e., before he had this experience, Mani had
been — like his father Patek before him — a member of the Jewish
Christian Elkesaite sect in Babylonia.

The new discovery not only confirms the most recent theories
about the origins of Gnosticism; it also seems to coincide with the
latest findings in the field of Syrian Church history.

Not long ago we discovered that, in contrast to Mediterranean
Christianity of the Greek and Latin variety, neither the origins
nor the essence of Aramaic Christianity had ever been catholic.
The historical picture is therefore very clearcut: a Latin form of
Christianity, which was practical and legalistic, wrestling with sin
and atonement, strove to establish a theocratic world order through
the medium of the papacy. This form subsequently gave rise to
Roman Catholicism and later to Protestantism. Furthermore, there
was Greek, ontological Christianity, which was concerned with the
synthesis of being and time, thus creating an impressive type of
Christology. Its heirs are the Slavic Churches and the Monophysitic
Churches of Egypt, Ethiopia and Armenia. In addition, however,
there was Aramaic Christianity, whose center was in Edessa and
which lives on in the Thomas Christians of India and in other
remnants of Nestorianism. This was a pluriform and colourful kind
of Christianity, whose adepts could be found among the wandering
and the poor (and as I pointed out earlier, it never was catholic).
The reason was that it did not have its origins in Gentile Christianity,
but in Palestinian Judaism.[2]

---

[1] Kölner Codex 24, 9-11; *cf.* Henrichs und Koenen, 168 f.

[2] G. Quispel, *Makarius, das Thomasevangelium und das Lied von der Perle,*
Leiden, 1967.

From Jean Cardinal Daniélou's contribution to *The Crucible of Christianity*, it becomes quite apparent that for a long time Christianity continued to exist as a Jewish sect, whose activities paralleled and even went counter to those of St. Paul. This sect was responsible for the beginnings of Christianity in Egypt, Carthage and Rome.[1] There, it was soon replaced by Gentile Christianity, but outside the Roman Empire, i.e., in Babylonia and Mesopotamia this was not the case. I fail to understand how scholars can possibly deny the Jewish Christian elements in Aramaic Christianity, especially since Hieronymus reported that in Aleppo he had visited Jewish Christians in the fourth century. According to him, they had not been hostile to the Church and had recognized Paul. However, they had their own gospel, the *Nazorean Gospel*, and adhered to Jewish law. On the other hand, the *Gospel of Thomas*, written in neighbouring Edessa around 140 A.D., proves that the Nazoreans had existed in Mesopotamia much earlier, as it contains elements of Jewish Christian Gospel tradition.[2]

Moreover, Hippolytus reported that the Jewish Christian prophet Elkesai had a vision in Parthia around 100 A.D.[3] At that time, Babylonia, where millions of Jews lived, belonged to the Parthian Empire. It can therefore be assumed that Elkesai was active in Babylonia, and as a result, it thus becomes understandable how Mani happened to grow up among the Elkesaites in southern Babylonia.

In addition, there were also Encratites in Mesopotamia. They rejected marriage, the drinking of wine, the eating of meat and held other unusual ideas. We know them from the Encratitic *Logia* in the *Gospel of Thomas*, the *Acts of Thomas*, as well as from Tatian's *Diatessaron*, which was written in Mesopotamia around 170 A.D. The brilliant scholar Erik Peterson[4] rightly saw in these

---

[1] J. Daniélou, 'That the Scripture might be fulfilled'. Christianity as a Jewish Sect, in *The Crucible of Christianity*, ed. by A. Toynbee, London, 1969, 261-282.

[2] G. Quispel, *Het Evangelie van Thomas en de Nederlanden*, Amsterdam, 1971.

[3] Hippolytus, *Refutatio*, IX, 13.

[4] E. Peterson, Bemerkungen zum hamburger Papyrusfragment der Acta Pauli, in *Frühkirche, Judentum und Gnosis*, Rom- Freiburg-Wien, 1951, 204 ff.

Encratites the founders of Manichaeism, although in developing this thesis he made a mistake. According to tradition, Mani's father heard in the heathen temple: "Patik, do not eat meat, drink no wine and abstain from women", and this led Peterson to conclude that the Baptists, to whom Mani and his father belonged, were Encratites. However, there is no reason to believe that the Elkesaites were ascetics. Other scholars, who erroneously identified these Baptists with the non-ascetic Mandaeans, made tremendous scholarly efforts to prove that the Mandaeans had indeed been ascetics at one time, although it is eminently clear that these words did not refer to any historical facts, but were simply an expression of tendentious Manichaean propaganda. On the other hand, Peterson was quite correct in pointing out that it would be difficult to explain Mani's experience with the Twin without the *Acts of Thomas* (in which Thomas is looked upon as Jesus' twin), or even the Manichaean condemnation of sexual intercourse without the influence of the Encratites.[1]

Inasmuch as the religious life of Edessa was by no means monolithic, mention must also be made of Bardesanes. There are many conflicting notions regarding the original doctrine of this highly gifted man. In any event, he taught the pre-existence of matter, a theory that must have been known to Mani.

It is impossible to prove that the Mesopotamian Christians also included Marcionites and Gnostics. Yet, we must assume that this was so, because Marcion must have been the premise for Mani's and his disciple Addai's criticism of the *Old Testament* and because the name Mani gave to the Creator of Man, Saclas, i.e., the Fool, presupposes the myth of the *Apocryphon of John*.

In visualizing Aramaic Christianity as it existed in those days, one could easily imagine that the founding of the Manichaean religion meant little more for its author than Erik Peterson's or Heinrich Schlier's "conversion", i.e., simply a transition from one

---

[1] G. Quispel, Das ewige Ebenbild des Menschen. Zur Begegnung mit dem Selbst in der Gnosis, *Eranos Jahrbuch* 36, 1967, 23 ff.,

variety of Christianity to another. In so far as they can be ascer-
tained clearly, any Buddhist or Iranian elements in the Manichaean
system are completely secondary. This applies in particular to
Manichaean dualism.

The ideas of the Elkesaites are fairly well-known to us from the
Pseudo-Clementine Homilies, and they are strikingly Jewish. In these
writings, everything is concretized. The eschatology is concrete: the
kingdom of Heaven is to be realized on earth. The concept of God
is concrete: God is considered a figure and not an idea or a principle.
Thus, even evil was viewed realistically as one of God's creatures
and not as a *privatio boni* or as matter. Satan is described as having
been created out of a mixture of the elements and as a servant of
God, his "left" hand.[1] It was a very courageous and consistent
form of monotheism, which can also be found in the *Old Testament*
as well as the *Dead Sea Scrolls,* and which has remained characteristic of Jewish mysticism. As the Clementine Gospel quotations
show, the Elkesaites placed strong emphasis on this concept.

All Matthew (10:29) said was that no sparrow falls to the ground
without God — an expression which provides the possibility of
side-stepping the issue. The pseudo-Clementines were much more
radical in saying that no sparrow is caught in a snare without the
will of God (XII, 31). Even the tragic fate of a helpless bird caught
through human meanness is attributed to the will of God. In the
Pseudo-Clementine Homilies (XII,29) Jesus says:

> That which is good must be brought about
> And blessed is he, who brings it about.
> That which is evil has to come about
> But woe onto him, who brings it about.

In history both good and evil occur, because God so wills it. These
same quotations, as so many others of Jewish Christian origin,
can also be found in Mani's own or other Manichaean writings for
the simple reason that Mani grew up in a Jewish Christian community and took over a number of sayings that did not coincide

---

[1] *Ps. Clem. Homiliae,* XX, 3,6.

with his own convictions. His only real concern was to prove that
God was not responsible for the bird being caught in the snare,
i.e., for the occurrence of evil in the history of man.

Tertullian once said that Marcion and many others, especially
heretics, who struggled with the question of *unde malum*, were
induced to postulate a better God upon reading the following
words of God in Isaiah: "Ego sum, qui condo mala" (*Adv. Marc.* I,2).
This is undoubtedly the existential core of the problem in man that
gave rise to Gnosticism. Moreover, as shown by the *Pseudo-Clementines*, it should be recalled that the Elkesaites' view hardened
in the course of their struggle against Marcion. In other words,
Mani did not militate against Christianity in general or against
Catholicism, but against this specific Jewish Christian doctrine.
Time and again he condemns the idea that God is the source of
evil. According to him, evil is the "non-thing" which God did
not want, but which will forever exist side by side with Him.
Manichaean dualism is Mani's reaction against the Jewish Christian
faith of his youth. Even he postulated, however, that the original
antithesis was not light and darkness, but God and Satan and he,
too, held that Satan was created out of the primordial elements, which
shows that he was unable to escape the influence of his opponent.
To understand Mani's attitude toward Christianity, it must be
remembered that his canon differed from ours. It is a fact that he
did not recognize the *Acts of Luke*, but on the other hand considered
the so-called apocryphal acts of the apostles to be canonical. Let us
not forget that the *Acts of Thomas* originated in Edessa around 225
in Encratitic circles. However, the *Acts of John* also had a strong
influence on him and contributed to the development of the doctrine
of *Jesus patibilis*. For, in the *Acts of John*, Christ says that he
suffers with all those who are suffering innocently.[1] The beginning
of his *Epistula Fundamenti* shows that Mani had knowledge of the
Gospel of Thomas. On the other hand it is not known who transmitted the letters of Paul to him.

---

[1] *Acta Johannis*, 96.

The most important thing that should be remembered is that
most probably he did not know the canonical gospels, for the simple
reason that in those days and for a long time to come Tatian's
Diatessaron was the recognized gospel of Aramaic Christianity.
We have no evidence that translations of the gospels existed in
Edessa at that time or anywhere in the Persian Empire, where
Mani used to live. In contrast, the Manichaean fragments prove
that Mani both knew and used Tatian's *Diatessaron*.[1] This
must be taken into consideration in attempting to answer the
question about Mani's attitude toward Christianity.

A number of Manichaean witnesses claimed that Jesus said he
would send the Holy Spirit to mankind. Thus, St. Augustine quotes
the Manichaean Felix as follows: *mittam vobis Spiritum Sanctum
Paracletum* (I,2). According to the Cologne Papyrus, Mani himself
said: Κύριος ἀπέστειλέν μοι σύξυγον (The Lord sent me a
partner) (p. 120). In the An-Nadim's *Fihrist* the "Twin" says to
Mani: Greetings to you, Mani, from myself and the Lord, who has
sent me to you and has chosen you for His mission (Flügel, *Mani*,
p. 84). It had always been assumed that this was an allusion to the
Gospel according to John (14:16). It should, however, be noticed that
the wording in the Fourth Gospel is different: And I will pray the
Father, and *he* shall *give* you another Paraclete (14:16). On the
basis of Ephrem Syrus' Commentary on the *Diatessaron*, we have
evidence that Tatian actually changed this wording, because he
did not read: "He shall give", but "I shall send". According to
Tatian's view, Christ himself would send the Paraclete. This was
what Mani read in his copy of the *Diatessaron* and it aquired
fundamental importance for him.

Mani's religious experience was not in fact unique. Encounters
with the Self as a guardian angel can also be found in Valentinian
Gnosticism as well as in Jewish and Islamic mysticism.[2] The Greeks,
especially the Pythagoreans, conceived of the *daimon* as the

---

[1] C. Peters, *Das Diatessaron Tatians* Orientalia Christiana Analecta 123, Rom.
1939, 125 ff.

[2] G. Quispel, Das ewige Ebenbild des Menschen, *Eranos Jahrbuch* 36, 1967, 9-20.

counterpart image of man's Self. This idea was taken over by Judaism and thus crept into Jewish and Syrian Christianity. In the *Gospel of Thomas* it is of central importance. Moreover, it is a notion that is found not only in religion but also in literature, such as German Romanticism and in the poems of the Dutch poet A. Roland Holst. It is a recurrent *topos* in history. The encounter with one's own Self does not seem to be a rare occurrence. The unique and important aspect of Mani's religious experience was that he thought his Self to be the Paraclete and that on the basis of Tatian's *Diatessaron* he was able to give his experience a Christian interpretation.

The title "Apostle of Jesus Christ", which Mani applied to himself, should also be viewed against this background. The fact that he used it was neither an attempt at imitation, nor a pretext but resulted from true conviction. Mani assumed the name of Apostle because he interpreted his Twin as the Paraclete and because he had read in Tatian that Christ would send the Paraclete. Augustine pointed out quite correctly that:

> "Unde se in suis litteris Jesu Christi apostolum dicit eo quod *Jesus Christus* se *missurum* esse promiserit atque in illo miserit spiritum sanctum."(*De haeresibus*, 46) (In his letters he therefore styles himself as Apostle of Jesus Christ because Jesus Christ promised he would send him and in him he sent the Holy Spirit.)

Mani's understanding of the Self can be properly evaluated only on the basis of this statement in Tatian. He did not indulge in self-deification; not his empirical ego, but his transcendental Self was the Paraclete.

On the other hand there can be no doubt that Mani himself interpreted the Twin as the Paraclete mentioned in John, despite the attempts that were made time and again to question this interpretation. As early as 1734 Isaac de Beausobre wrote that Mani had never claimed to be the Paraclete (*Histoire du Manichéisme* I, 103). The extent to which phenomenology and the history of religion have failed to make any progress in the last 250 years is shown in the work of L. J. R. Ort, who, despite the lack of any evidence or knowledge of the *Diatessaron*, claimed that the title of Paraclete for Mani was an invention of Western Manichaeism, an assimilation to Christianity for missionary purposes.[1] Tatian's variant, which was known to Mani, however, disproves these theories.

There is no reason to assume, as Geo Widengren did in his book on Mani, that a Buddhist shrine existed in Seleukia-Ktesifon, that there was an ascetic trend in Mandaeism, that the incarnation of the divine Self was of Iranian origin, or that there had been a Mandaean period in Mani's life, not to mention the theory of a substratum of the old Mesopotamian religion as it manifested itself in Gnostic Baptism — suppositions which are all without foundations.[2] A careful reading of the Fourth Gospel will prove much more enlightening.

Mani, however, owes still another of the doctrines he followed to Jewish Christianity. According to the *Pseudo-Clementines*, Jesus was the true Prophet. On the other hand, the true Prophet had already appeared before. The Holy Spirit had incarnated itself earlier in Adam and later revealed itself to the patriarchs of the *Old Testament*, such as Abraham and Moses, until, having appeared in varying shapes over a period of centuries, it came to rest in Jesus. Mani took up this idea and amplified it. According to him, Buddha, Zarathustra as well as Jesus were sent out to different nations at different times as emanations of the same principle that manifested itself with finality and perfection in Mani, the Paraclete.

Mani's dualism as well as his doctrine of the successive incarnations can therefore be explained on the basis of his Jewish Christian background.

This throws some new and unexpected light on the origins of Islam. Mohammed's concept of his mission had always appeared to bear a striking resemblance to the Jewish Christian concept of

---

[1] L. J. R. Ort, *Mani. A religio-historical description of his personality*, Leiden, 1967, 259.

[2] G. Widengren, *Mani und der Manichäismus*, Stuttgart, 1961.

the true Prophet. Not only was Jesus, according to him, a prophet like other prophets before him, but Mohammed himself was the true and final Prophet, the Seal of the Prophets. Until recently, it had not been possible to find any evidence of Mohammed's connection with Jewish Christianity. It had been assumed that the Jewish Christians had lived exclusively in Transjordania and had gradually become extinct. Owing to the discovery of the *Cologne Codex,* we now know, however, that southern Babylonia had also been inhabited by Elkesaites, who had called themselves Baptists, because after the actual baptism, they practised certain additional ablutions for the purification and atonement of their sins.

Baptists (Sabians) were mentioned in the Koran in three places (II,59; V,73; XXII,17) as members of a recognized religion of the Book, which, according to Mohammed's precepts, was to be tolerated along with Judaism and Christianity. It is too early to make any definitive statement in this matter, because the whole problem will have to be investigated by a scholar specialized in Islamic studies. But as a working hypothesis we are quite justified in assuming even now that these Sabians, the Baptists of the Koran, should be identified with the Jewish Christian Elkesaites. This would mean that Mohammed was acquainted both with the existence and the views of the Jewish Christians. The parallelism in concept regarding the true Prophet would thus have to be attributed to Jewish Christianity's historically verifiable influence on Mohammed. In this context it should also be recalled that, just like Islam, Jewish Christianity is basically a legalistic religion, which remained faithful to Jewish law, although it recognized Jesus as the Messiah of the Jewish people. If one follows this line of thought, it becomes much more apparent that it was actually St. Paul who cast Christianity as a faith with freedom from law and as a religion of the spirit. Paul's true greatness comes to light only when viewed in this perspective. For, the actual dialogue between Christianity on the one hand, and Islam, as well as Judaism on the other, should be concerned with Paul's concept of the Law.

It also comes as somewhat of a surprise to see how fertile and productive Jewish Christianity was in Asia. In a sense, it gave rise to two religions, i.e., Manichaeism and Islam, which, looked at in this perspective, become Christian heresies.

Moreover, it also becomes completely clear to what extent the theses developed by the so-called School of the History of Religion were wrong. Reitzenstein, in his time, used Manichaeism as a point of departure in order to explain that Gnosticism and Christianity had Iranian origins. In a Manichaean fragment he found a dialogue between the Ego and the Self and decided that it must be Iranian. Hereafter, he was certain that both Mandaeism and Manichaeism were purely Iranian and that these religions should be used to explain Christianity, which after all was more than 200 years older. The premise for this assertion was, of course, that Mani had spent his early years among the Mandaeans.

Geo Widengren set out to prove these extravagant hypotheses with great thoroughness. According to him, Manichaeism was a mixture of Mesopotamian and Iranian religions. He claimed that the doctrine of the Prophet originated in Mesopotamia and that the idea of a succession of prophets stemmed from Iran. Widengren was convinced that before Mani's time both views had been merged in Gnostic Mandaeism, to which Mani was supposed to have belonged.

In the meantime, the story transmitted by the Arabian writer An-Nadim was systematically neglected. According to An-Nadim, Mani never belonged to the Mandaean sect in his youth but to the Jewish Christian sect of the Elkesaites.[1] This was also confirmed by the *Cologne Codex*. One must ask oneself, whether a science that dares to drop written tradition by the wayside to follow up valueless fantasies is really worth the name. We now know that as a child Mani was a Jewish boy, that he was circumcised and celebrated the Sabbath. Indeed, it must even be doubted that his parents were of Parthian and royal origin, a fact that was mentioned by An-Nadim, but not in the *Cologne Codex*. Most probably this

---

[1] G. Flügel, *Mani, seine Lehre und seine Schriften*, Osnabrück, 1969 (= Nachdruck der Ausgabe 1862), 133.

was a legend which arose out of the desire to rediscover in the person of Mani the Parthian prince mentioned in the *Song of the Pearl*.

Mani was a Jewish Christian. For this reason, his basic experience, the encounter with the Self, should be explained against this background. In this case, it should, however, also be possible to understand the fundamental concepts of Manichaeism, the identity of the ego and the self, the empirical ego and the guardian angel, in terms of his Jewish Christian origins. We would thus have to interpret Manichaeism, a religion without sacraments, as a spiritualization of Jewish Christian baptism.

II

I wonder whether at Eranos I even dare mention Christian baptism. I suppose that it is somewhat risky, but in order to understand the early Christian baptismal tradition, you will have to forget everything Karl Barth wrote in his Dogmatics about baptism. Karl Barth not only claimed that child christening was nonsense but that baptism was not a sacrament at all. An assertion of this kind is incomprehensible to anyone who knows the documents of the Early Church or even just the New Testament. Perhaps we should also forget all that has been said in the West about baptism, for we must remember that all such statements were subject to the influence of St. Augustine, who thought that baptism absolves us from original sin and the primordial guilt of concupiscence. This concept is very interesting but was little known in the Christian Church in the centuries preceding St. Augustine. One might conjecture that Augustine was indebted to Manichaeism for this notion, as he had been a Manichaean himself for over nine years. There actually are some indications to this effect, but I shall not dwell on them in this context. We therefore have to delve a little further into the past and ask what the Early Christians taught about baptism and how they practiced it. We soon realize that the concept of rebirth coincided with that of baptism. In other words, in the view of the Early Church the inner event of a new birth coincided with the outer ritual of baptism. It is important to remember this in order to understand the purpose and the deeper meaning which the Christians attributed to baptism and rebirth.

The Early Gentile Church engaged in a whole series of rituals, beautiful and highly symbolic acts which were not entirely archaic. People were immersed three times in the name of the Father, the Son and the Holy Ghost, whereupon the venue of the Holy Ghost was called down upon them by the imposition of the hands. This cannot have been the original concept and to discover it, we might do well to disregard even the views of St. Paul on this matter.

You all know that in *Romans* 6, Paul expressed very profound views about the nature of baptism. You will recall that for Paul Christ's death and resurrection were almost more important than His life. His views of Christian baptism have to be regarded against this background. We might summarize them in Goethe's words:

"Until you have grasped this—Die and be transformed!— You will be nothing but a sorry guest on the sombre earth." (*Selige Sehnsucht*)

While Paul would have agreed with this entirely, "die and be transformed" would also have meant to him the outer ritual act of baptism. For, according to Paul, baptism is a form of death, a submersion in water and a re-emergence, i.e., a resurrection in union with Christ and in Christ. In *Romans* 6, Paul said that when we are baptized into union with Christ Jesus we are baptized into His death, immersed in it; and he clearly stated that the sacrament of the holy baptism is an image of Christ's death. Thus, whenever an initiate is immersed in water and re-emerges, the image of Christ's death is re-enacted in him.

Paul's concept inevitably brings to mind the Greek mysteries, because in many of them — irrespective of whether they were devoted to Osiris, Attis or Adonis — a young god who embodies living nature dies and is reborn. A great deal has been written about the relationship between the Greek mysteries and the

Christian sacraments. I do not intend to go into the matter, but simply want to point out that in describing the holy baptism as an image of death Paul is using the language of the Greek mysteries. The mysteries of Adonis, for instance, were looked upon as an image of Adonis' death. The mythical event of the young god's death was ritually re-enacted during every celebration of the mystery. The very expression "image of death" used to refer to the mysteries of Adonis. Ovid used it in describing the death of Osiris and the mourning women: "repetitaque mortis imago annua plangoris peraget simulamina nostri (the image of the death is re-enacted annually by the celebration of our sorrow)."[1]

The expression used in relation to the Adonis mysteries is therefore the same as that used by Paul in his Epistle to the Romans: the mystery of baptism as an image of Christ's death; Christ in his death and resurrection must therefore be assumed to have been present at the baptism in the same manner as Adonis was presumed to have been present at the mysteries. Along with Hugo Rahner, who discussed this topic so eloquently at *Eranos*, I therefore do not preclude the possibility that, in writing about baptism Paul may have been using the language of the Greek mysteries.[2] This does not help us, however, in our investigations of Jewish Christian baptism. You undoubtedly know that the Jewish Christians differed from Paul precisely in that for them it was not Christ's death which brought salvation, although they recognized His ressurrection. The Jewish Christian source material says nothing about baptism being associated with Christ's death. Furthermore, it is extremely difficult for us to imagine that these Palestinian Christians — very humble people living in Transjordania — had been influenced by the Greek mysteries. We shall see, however, that their ideas regarding the mystery to a large extent paralleled those of the Greeks.

---

[1] Ovid, *Metam.*, X, 726-727.

[2] H. Rahner, *Griechische Mythen in christlicher Deutung*, 3. Aufl., Darmstadt, 1966, 19-54.

I would tend to agree with Odo Casel, who repeatedly emphasized this point in his study of the sacraments as the Christian mysteries. According to him, Christianity was not influenced by the Greek mysteries to any great extent. Yet, according to Casel, the cult *eidos* of the Christian sacrament — the idea that the rite was a re-enactment of the original myth — was quite comparable to the cult *eidos* of the Greek mysteries. A rather ingenious mind once formulated the idea as follows: Christianity was not influenced by the Greek mysteries precisely because in its origin and essence it was already a mystery religion. I would be inclined to accept this definition, provided, however, that Jewish Christian baptism is viewed as a product of Judaism and that form of Christianity which was based on Judaism. Jean Cardinal Daniélou and Georg Kretschmar provided us with detailed studies describing the original Jewish Christian baptismal rites.[1] From the works of these learned scholars we infer that this form of baptism was not characterized by simplicity. On the contrary, it was apparently much more complex, meaningful and symbolic than our present-day baptism. There is no doubt that Jewish Christian baptism had a deeply spiritual, symbolic content. These people lived in a symbolic world and, as Gershom Scholem pointed out, in a period when a break-through of images occurred in Jewish culture. In fact all aspects of Jewish Christian baptism are related to Judaism; not to the Rabbinical or Pharisaic variety, of course, but to heterodox forms of Judaism. I am thinking here of the Essenes or the Baptists (followers of John the Baptist), a hitherto wholly unknown aspect of Judaism which was discovered only quite recently.

The origins of baptism are entirely Jewish. The Essenes practiced ablutions which probably influenced the Jewish Christians. Christian baptism is therefore not only highly symbolic and mythological, it is also very Jewish. As erudite scholars have discussed this topic at length, I shall confine myself to a very brief description of the

---

[1] J. Daniélou, *Théologie du judéo-christianisme*, Tournai, 1958, 369-386.
G. Kretschmar, *Die Geschichte des Taufgottesdienstes in der alten Kirche*, in *Leiturgia*, V, Kassel, 1970 (= 1964), 14-58.

baptismal rites performed in those days. Among other things, baptism was required to take place in "living" water, i.e., a spring, a river, especially the Jordan, or the sea. Even much later, the baptismal water was frequently referred to merely as "the Jordan". The *datio salis*, the giving of salt, which continues to be a Roman Catholic rite today, is undoubtedly of Jewish origin, too, because we now have evidence that the salt was considered to be essential to the covenant aspect of baptism. However, I shall refrain from giving you any further examples and simply provide you with a schematic outline of the probable course of events.

Baptism for the absolution of sins existed even prior to Jesus as evidenced by the story of John the Baptist. This concept of baptism is thus pre-Christian. On the other hand, the words of John the Baptist "He will baptize you with the Holy Spirit" show that the Spirit was added as a new element. This was the content of Jewish Christian baptism, whereas the profound interpretation symbolizing death and resurrection must be attributed to Paul and his co-Hellenists.

After this brief outline I shall now discuss three aspects of Jewish Christian baptism, i.e., anointment, rebirth and the bridal chamber.

In contrast to the practices of the western Gentile Church, anointment preceded the actual baptismal bath in the rites of the Jewish Christians as well as the Syrian Christians, whose practices evolved out of those of their Jewish brethren. Some passages in the *New Testament* (*Acts* 10:44; *Cor.* 10:2) imply that this rite existed in the early Christian era. What does this mean ? The Jewish Christians believed that Jesus became Christ at His baptism. A number of present-day occult sects continue to hold this view, but it is very ancient and originated with the Jewish Christians. Jesus was believed to have become the Messiah, because during His baptism the Holy Spirit descended upon Him. Messiah, of course, means the Anointed One. On the one hand, what took place here was a spiritualization of the Jewish Messiah ideal, the Anointed One being he who was anointed with the Holy Spirit. On the other, it explains to us why anointment became part of the baptismal ritual. For, to lead a Christian existence according to the Jewish Christian concept, one had to follow in Christ's footsteps and even imitate his life. In describing the baptism of Jesus, the *Jewish Christian Gospel* says: "My Son Thou art, ... this day I have begotten Thee." This notion was taken over by the Syrian Christians, whose priests say to the initiate while anointing him: "My Son Thou art, this day I have begotten Thee." Through baptism man became God's child; this was expressed by the practice of anointing the entire body of the Christian adept prior to his baptism.

We know a great deal about this custom as it was practised in Syria. However, we also know that it existed among the Jewish Christians of Palestine, who even went so far as to call themselves *Christoi*, i.e., the Anointed Ones. They did not mean to imply that they resembled the Messiah in every respect, but they believed that, in *imitatio* of him, they were anointed with the Holy Spirit. The Holy Spirit descended to earth when Jesus became Christ at His baptism and this has been repeated in the lives of all initiates ever since.[1]

The ceremony of anointment is well known from the Old Testament, where we read of kings, priests and prophets being anointed. As a result of anointment one becomes a king, priest, or prophet. All these notions are embodied in the ritual of anointment and it is difficult to differentiate between them. One might say that, since Christ was the true prophet for the Jewish Christians, every Christian must possess a prophetic quality. This idea cannot be dissociated from the Christians' belief that they were a people of kings and priests. This belief is the fulfillment of God's word to Moses, which according to the Bible foretold that the Jews "shall be unto Me a Kingdom of priests and a holy nation." (Exodus 19:6). The meaning of anointment can only be understood in the Jewish perspective. The Christian innovation was that anyone, even the humble and the poor, could be anointed. Using a rather

---

[1] Hippolytus, *Refutatio*, VII, 34,2.

controversial but unavoidable expression, we would have to call
it the democratization caused by the advent of Christianity. I am
quite aware of the fact that democracy is a loaded word. Usually
I try to avoid it in my lectures, but at times it seems to be impossible. In this case, we have to admit that Early Christianity
had a democratic quality owing to the fact that even the humblest
person was able to receive the Holy Spirit and to belong to the
kingdom of priests. There were other non-Christian religious
movements in antiquity that reserved the mysteries for the spiritual
elite. Now anointment came to mean that anyone could have
access to the Spirit.

In Iraq and Iran the Mandaeans have survived as a sect to this
day, and it is highly probable that they continue to practice the
form of baptism advocated by John the Baptist. Very scholarly
investigations have shown that anointment was not originally a
Mandaean practice.[1] As far as we can tell, it is of no importance to
them. In this connection, I am always reminded of the Baptist's
word regarding Jesus: "I have baptized you with water"—which
is the customary practice among the Mandaeans—"He will baptize
you with the Holy Spirit", which is expressed in the symbolism
of anointment.

In addition, baptism is also the mystery of rebirth. It involves
absolution from sin and liberation from concupiscence. According
to the Pseudo-Clementines, the essential meaning of baptism is,
however, that man becomes a heir of his parents. This was misinter-
preted to mean that the sacrament of rebirth enlightened man
about his origins, existence and future. In actual fact, man comes
to know his divine origin; both his Father, i.e., God, as well as his
Mother. This point is made very clear in one passage of the *Pseudo-
Clementines* where it is stated that man shall know his parents —
gennesantes — i.e., God and the Mother.[2] Again, we cannot help but

---

[1] E. Segelberg, *Maṣbuta. Studies in the ritual of the Mandaean Baptism*, Uppsala
1958, 130 ff.

[2] *Homiliae*, XI, 24, 2.

be astounded, because we had always thought of Christianity as a thoroughly patriarchal religion. Now, it turns out that originally this was not so.

The Jewish Christians were entirely convinced that the Holy Spirit was a feminine hypostasis. A fragment from the Jewish Christian Gospels reads as follows: "Even so did my Mother, the Holy Spirit, take me by one of my hairs and carry me away onto the great mountain Tabor." In another fragment, the Holy Spirit says to Jesus at his baptism: "My Son, in all the prophets I was waiting for Thee."[1] The idea expressed in these passages was that Jesus was reborn at His baptism which for Him, too, was the bath of rebirth. Every Jewish Christian should therefore be thought of as having been reborn by his mother the Holy Spirit after emerging from complete immersion in the baptismal bath. Here, we come to a very simple realization: just as birth requires a mother, so rebirth requires a spiritual mother. Originally, the Christian term "rebirth" must therefore have been associated with the concept of the spirit as a feminine hypostasis.

Let us reflect on what this implies. In the *Gospel according to John*, Jesus says to Nicodemus: "In truth, in very truth I tell you, unless a man has been born over again he cannot see the kingdom of God." (John 3:3) The same wording can also be found in the *Pseudo-Clementines*. Since they were not acquainted with the Fourth Gospel, these words are clearly taken from a free Palestinian tradition. Actually the Pseudo-Clementine wording is much simpler: "Unless you are reborn, you shall not enter the kingdom of Heaven."[2] The Jewish Christians, therefore, also handed down these words of Jesus as part of their tradition. They seem to have believed that a rebirth was a true act of procreation, a birth by the Holy Spirit. I cannot escape the notion that this may have been the original meaning of Christ's word.

---

[1] E. Hennecke, *New Testament Apocryphs*, Engl. translation by R. Mc. L. Wilson, London, 1963, p. 164.

[2] *Homiliae*, XI, 26, 2.

The re-enactment of birth in a mystery inevitably brings to mind the Greek mysteries, although the idea is not always rendered in the same manner. It has been pointed out that in the blood baptism of the Attis mysteries the expression *renatus in aeternum*, reborn in eternity, was used, but blood baptism does not signify a birth by a mother. It may well be that in this respect the Attis mysteries were influenced by Christianity.

Apuleius mentioned the fact that he was, as it were, reborn, *quodam modo renatus*, when he was initiated into the Isis mysteries.[1] According to his reports, this initiation in no way involved birth by a mother, but referred to a cosmic experience, which is a rebirth only in a metaphorical sense.

The only parallel I know of can be found in the Eleusinian mysteries, although no historical connection can be established with the Christian tradition. Recent research into the Eleusinian mysteries uncovered some important material. I should like to draw your attention to a specific action and a vision which formed a part of these mysteries.

It seems that, after the fast and after having drunk the *kykeon*, the mystes took something out of a large basket, then performed "the act"and replaced "the something" in the basket. The reference is very mysterious. What was in the basket? Even in antiquity some people seemed to have thought that it was a phallus. However, Theodoretus reported that the basket in the Eleusinian mysteries contained a womb.[2] A. Körte assumed that the mystes passed the womb under his garments, then dropped it on the ground and replaced it in the basket: a very peculiar rite, which can probably be interpreted as an adoption rite.[3] According to a Greek author, Diodorus Siculus, (V, 39), Hera at one time adopted Heracles as her son by pressing him against her body and then dropping him on the ground to simulate a birth. We must therefore assume that this strange gesture should be understood as an adoption rite.

---

[1] Apuleius, *Metam.*, XI, 16, 4.

[2] Theodoretus von Kyros, *Graec. aff. cur.*, VII, 11.

[3] A. Körte, *Archiv für Religionswissenschaft*, 18, 1915, 119.

In my view such an interpretation would explain the mysterious words belonging to the Orphic doctrine which were inscribed on a gold tablet found in southern Italy. On it we read: "I have sunk beneath the bosom of Despoina, the Queen of the Underworld." Probably this meant that, in death, the author of these words, an Orphic, was adopted by the Goddess of the Underworld, i.e., Persephone. He thus became a child of the chthonic Mother. As the vision in Eleusis seems to indicate, the mystes is adopted as a child of the divine mother through the performance of this rite, which constitutes a valid parallel to Jewish Christian baptism. Evoking the ineffable holy thing, the Hierophant proclaimed in a loud voice: "The Mistress has given birth to a holy boy. Brimo has given birth to Brimos, that is, the Strong One to the Strong One." In his vision the mystes evidently saw the birth of the child from the Earth Goddess, and by re-enacting the mystery, he must have felt that somehow he had become the child of the Mother.

We should by no means draw the conclusion that the Jewish Christians were influenced by the Eleusinian mysteries. The symbolism developed spontaneously. The *Pseudo-Clementines* said that in the beginning the Spirit hovered over the waters, and inasmuch as everything was created out of water and Spirit, the Spirit or Mother also created man anew by hovering over the baptismal waters. The premise for this statement is, of course, that the Holy Spirit is feminine.[1]

Finally, brief reference should be made to the bridal chamber. This custom seems to have been practiced by the Valentinians, as well as the Manichaeans, and we find mention of it in the recently discovered *Gospel of Philip*, written by a Valentinian in Antioch around 200 B.C. It is unlikely that the ceremony of the bridal chamber is of Gnostic origin, because it is also part of Syrian Church practices. It should probably be attributed to Jewish Christianity, for in the *Pseudo Clementines* we read: "When illuminated by the Spirit and sown with the True Prophet's White Word

---

[1] *Homiliae*, XI, 26, 3.

of Truth, every human being is a bride."[1] Once a person has been baptized a new symbol has been enacted and the man or woman becomes a bride. We find here another strange parallel, this time to the Mithras mysteries. In these mysteries it was traditional for the initiate to have the following lines sung to him: "Sing oh *nymphĕ*, rejoice oh *nymphĕ*, rejoice oh new light." Scholars used to argue a great deal about the meaning of the Greek word *nymphĕ*. Some people even wanted to change it to *nymphios*, bridegroom, until it was found that the initiates in the Mithras mysteries, who were all men, were conceived of as male brides. Once again, we should not conclude that the Mithras mysteries influenced Jewish Christianity. Both traditions simply developed the same imagery. We do not actually know how the scene was enacted by the Jewish Christians. The *Gospel of Philip* intimates that a bridal chamber was built, to which the new adept was led after his or her baptism. Here, the holy nuptial, the *mysterium coniunctionis*, took place. One can hardly help thinking that the rite symbolized the union of the soul with Christ. There is undoubtedly some connection here, but the *Gospel of Philip* tells us that, in the mystery of the bridal chamber, man is joined in marriage to his Guardian Angel, who is the Self. No doubt the true content of this mystery is man's union, the *mysterium coniunctionis*, with his Guardian Angel, his *Daimon*, or the Self. I do not think we can exclude the possibility that this concept goes back to Jewish Christian tradition. The fact is that in Jewish Christian baptism the initiate wears a white garment, which is after all a symbol of the Self, points to a union of the existential Ego with the spiritual Self, not eschatologically, but in the here and now. For, both the guardian angel and the heavenly robe can symbolize the transcendental Self.

I am therefore inclined to think that Mani's religious experience, his encounter with the Self, presupposes and spiritualizes the symbolism of anointment, rebirth and the *mysterium coniunctionis* of Jewish Christian baptism.

---

[1] *Homiliae*, III, 27, 3.

Gershom Scholem
Three Types of Jewish Piety

I.

Let me open by quoting a talmudic story. «Rabbi once opened his
storehouse of victuals in a year of scarcity, proclaiming: Let those enter
who have studied the Scripture, or the Mishnah or the Gemara or the
Halakha or the Aggada. There is no admission, however, for the ignorant. R. Jonathan ben Amram pushed his way in and said: Master,
give me food. He said: My son, have you learnt the Scripture? He
replied: No. Have you learnt the Mishnah? No? If so, he said, then
how can I give you food? He said to him: Feed me as the dog and the
raven are fed. So he gave him food. After he went away, Rabbi's con-
science smote him and he said: Woe to me that I have given my bread
to a man without learning. His son ventured to say to him: Perhaps
it is Jonathan ben Amram your pupil, who all his life has made it a
principle not to derive material benefit from the honour paid to the
Torah. Upon inquiry, it was found that it was so; whereupon Rabbi
said: All may now enter.»[1]

You can talk about a religion and its specific world in many ways.
You can describe or analyze its theology and dogma, that is to say its
teaching about God and Creation and the place of man in such a
scheme of things. You can also describe its ritual and way of life (Le-
bensordnung) and in particular I would say that often the liturgy, the
order of prayers and the life reflected in them serve as a true mirror to
the spiritual life of a religion. Some of the best works on Judaism or
Christianity have brought out the particular colour and life of such
groups by looking closely at liturgy. But this is not what I propose to

do this time. I wish to talk here about the basic attitudes, about the ideal human types which the history of rabbinic Judaism has evolved and I should like to discuss the tensions that are possible between them. The basic tension in the religious society of Judaism is that between rational and emotional factors, rational and irrational forces. The ideal types formed by this society will necessarily reflect such tension.

Let me put it in another way: How did the Jews see themselves, what were the ideal Jewish types of piety which Judaism knew in its classical forms over the last two thousand years? Such human types represent embodiments of a scale of values or of more or less independent highest values which have been put as an example to imitate or to strive for by other people. Such ideals of highest values realized in human lives will allow us an insight into what living Judaism meant for its people.

Now I do not think there can be any doubt as to what these types of the ideal Jew are. They are, if you allow me to use the popular Hebrew terms, *Talmid Hakham*, the rabbinic scholar, the *Zaddik*, the just Man, and the *Hasid*, a term which it is not easy to translate although its meaning will be made quite clear to us. Everybody has heard about these types in a more or less vague way, but we shall try to take a somewhat closer look at the meaning of each of them. Let me say at once that I am not discussing here biblical religion. I am discussing Judaism as constituted in its Talmudic and Rabbinical forms to which Jewish philosophy or, for that matter, Jewish mysticism have added other dimensions without basically changing its substance.

This is the reason why I am not talking in this context of the Prophet as an ideal type. Prophecy as seen in Judaism is not something for which you can prepare yourself, which you can make an ultimate aim of your way towards the realization of religion. The prophet is a man chosen by God for a mission to his people whatever his preparation or lack of preparation for such a mission may be. Neither can you educate your pupils for such a state nor can you set it as your own aim. It depends on something utterly beyond you, not to be foreseen and not to be sustained in a continuous frame of mind or as an attainment available *ad libitum*. You may argue that we hear about schools of prophets in old biblical times, but they have no relation to Judaism as an historical phenomenon as it has crystallized after the Babylonian exile. For the philosophers of Judaism, such as Maimonides, prophecy was indeed a highest spiritual state but not one to which we could aspire in our time and place. It was something belonging to the past, to the creative periods of Revelation, with other words: something belonging to biblical theology but not to the concrete requirements within the framework of our own life as Jews.

I mentioned in the first place the figure of the *Talmid Hakham*, the Rabbinic Scholar, or, as the extremely modest term would have to be translated literally: 'The Pupil of a Sage'. Now what is meant by this term? It is, above all, an intellectual value and a value of a life of contemplation. It has no essential relation to an emotional scale of values. What is asked from the scholar? A rational effort of the mind and its concentration. He is a student of scripture and tradition who has fully mastered the ways and means by which these two spheres, or should I say sources of the religious life of Judaism, are connected. Let us pause here for a moment. Judaism, like other religions based on the principle of revelation, has a canon, an established collection of sacred scripture, and the holy writ contains the truth about human life. The basic assumption of a religious constitution based on revelation and tradition, as historical Judaism obviously is, can be formulated in a simple and yet far reaching way which has profound implications of its own. *The truth is given and known once and for all.* It has not to be discovered. It has been laid down. The great task is to pass it on and to develop its meaning for every subsequent generation.

Modern man is prone to think highly of originality. Now, I would stress the fact that originality is not a value considered highly by the great religions. They do not think that truth has still to be discovered. It is there, in revelation, for all to see. It is the tremendous conflict between the modern and the traditionalist mind that they clash over this evaluation of originality and the discovery of truth. But even within the old framework, there is still immense room for the exercise of originality – but of an originality that does not acknowledge itself as such.

Rather does it hide behind the modest term of commentary as though there was nothing to do but to elicit and to develop what is laid down, perhaps only in a general way, in the documents of revelation.

The tradition of rabbinical Judaism constitutes a method to explore the meaning of Scripture. It has gone to great length, sometimes in a highly colourful and paradoxical way, to stress this point, namely, that whatever a decent and genuine scholar of Scripture can say about its meaning and application at any given time, has been hidden away somehow in Scripture itself and is a part of Revelation in its more general sense comprising what in Judaism is called the Oral Law, *Tora shebe'al Peh*. Let me illustrate this by a famous story in the Talmud told about Rabbi Akiba in the 2nd century, that is to say about a man who was always considered as the perfect embodiment of the type of which I am talking and who has done more than any other single great teacher in Judaism to bring about the crystallization of rabbinical Judaism into a system of extraordinary vitality. The story, for all its simplicity, is not without sublimity and depth and a twinkle of irony.

«When Moses ascended on high he found the Holy One, blessed be He, engaged in affixing coronets to the letters. Said Moses: Lord of the Universe, who stays thy hand? (that is to say: is there anything wanting in the Torah that these additions in the form of coronets are necessary?) He answered: There will arise a man, at the end of many generations, Akiba ben Joseph by name, who will expound on each tittle heaps and heaps of laws. Said Moses: Lord of the Universe, permit me to see him. He replied: Turn thee round. Moses went and sat down behind eight rows (of Akiba's disciples). But he was unable to understand their arguments and this made him alarmed (because he was unable to follow the discourses on the Torah given by himself); but when they came to a certain subject and the disciples said to the master: whence do you know this? and he replied: it is a teaching given unto Moses on Sinai, he was comforted. Thereupon he returned to the Holy One, Blessed be He, and said: Lord of the Universe, Thou hast such a man and thou givest the Torah by me? He replied: be silent, for such is my decree.'[2]

The genuine *Talmid Hakham*, in the eyes of tradition, cannot say anything utterly new, but only what was always known and contained in the source of revelation. His specific task in the world of Judaism is then a twofold one. First of all he brings out what was implied in the Torah, he is in full command of the art of reading and interpreting the sacred text. And secondly, he is able to apply this interpretation to the changing needs of the community. All this leads to one more point: the real sage who so modestly is called only a disciple of the sages, is the teacher of his community. His is not to be a prophetic quality; what is expected of him is not a novel revelation or truth of religion; the decisive quality expected of him is his sobriety and rationality by which he is able to expound the values that have come down and been held up by tradition, and his clarity of mind which makes him an educator, handing down those values to the next generation. He need not be ashamed to call himself what he is. We would think it pretty strange if somebody came along announcing: I am a Zaddik or: I am a Chasid, and the very statement would in our eyes disprove itself. But the Talmud says: If you come to a foreign place where you are not known, it is proper for you to say: I am a pupil of the sages. It is a measure of the sobriety of which I have spoken, of the reticence with which this type is described that for many generations in European Jewry the highest praise you could pay to somebody was the deceptively simple sentence 'Er kann lernen' (He knows how to learn). No more modest formula could be found in order to express the highest valuation. The little verb '*lernen*' (to learn) has an enormous implication. '*Lernen*' does not only mean studying but it means complete mastery of the Talmudist's world of intellectual tradition. He, about whom this can be said, is at the same time the teacher of his generation.

The scholar in the sense I tried to describe, is at the same time an aim of education, I might say the highest aim of education which the Jews have had over the last two thousand years of their history. I think it is a tremendous thing and speaks for the extraordinary vitality that has gone into the making of this type of Jew, that it has been able to maintain its unbroken power over such a period and in the face of all the vicissitudes of Jewish history. It is an ideal for which you can educate people and develop institutions that might produce it. And it is an

ideal that held equally for Jews wherever they lived, be it in Yemen or
Russia, in Babylonia or France. Even today the power of this ideal has
not been broken, although the last generations have made heavy in-
roads into the traditional ideals of Jewish life and we are witnessing
revolutionary changes, both in Israel and the Diaspora, which affect
the basis on which this life was built. But still, it might be said that the
number of students in Israel studying in the Yeshiva, that institution
which is intended to develop this particular ideal type, is approximately
as large as the number of students in the institutions of secular higher
learning. At the same time it is significant for the depth of the crisis in
which we live that to a great extent these institutions have ceased to
fulfil that central social function which was one of their greatest claims
to fame in our history. The *Talmid Hakham* as I have described him,
had a central social function in the Jewish community, he had authority in the world of tradition, but he did not evade his responsibility for
the application of the Old Torah in his own time. It is this evasion,
this shying away from taking on responsibility which is one of the more
distressing facets in the clash of ideals which we are witnessing now in
Israel.

I said that the figure of the *Talmid Hakham* had a deep rational
significance. But its aura has pervaded Jewish society far beyond rational limits. The magic of the names of the great representatives of this
type spread far and away and became household words to millions.
The Gaon of Vilna, or Rabbi Itzhak Elhanan, the Rav of Kovno, to
name only two outstanding figures, were such archetypal representatives of the ideal Talmid Hakham.

Controversy about the value of this phenomenon has not been lack-
ing since the first days of Christianity. It was open to attack, I might
even say it invited attack, from a more emotional point of view and
from those who sought the centre of religion and religious life in other
spheres of a more emotional character. It is not for me to take sides in
this discussion. What I want us to understand is the structure, the
build-up and the meaning of this type which, after all, has given to the
Jewish people that particular class of Intelligentsia for which they have
been, rightly or wrongly, praised or condemned.

II.

When we come to speak of the two other ideal types, the Zaddik and the Hasid, we enter a different sphere. The values represented by the 'pupil of the sages', the rabbinical scholar, belong, as I said before, to the sphere of contemplation. The scholar transfers himself into the world of the Torah which for him is a vehicle to a purely spiritual life. He studies actions, but he studies them not in their active quality, but he transforms them into subjects for contemplation, intellectual concentration and judicious penetration. The Zaddik and the Hasid, however, are not judged by the perfection of their intellectual penetration, but by the way they perform the discharge of their religious duties in action. They are, to put it short, ideals of the *active* life. Of course, the types are not exclusive of each other. A scholar may wellnigh be a Zaddik or a Hasid at the same time and vice versa. Each is to be judged by their own scale of values. If the *Talmid Hakham* represented an intellectual value in its perfection, the *Zaddik* or the *Hasid* represent what we would call ethical values, values of the heart and of the deeds of man.

In popular parlance and even in some parts of the old rabbinical sources there is no clear-cut distinction and separation between the two conceptions. There is a tendency to speak of the Zaddikim and to ascribe to them the widest range of virtues and qualities and very often the terms could be exchanged. The great figures of biblical literature are characterized almost throughout as Zaddikim, but on the other hand, if the Talmud tells some extraordinary story about a feat of religious performance, or a miracle vouchsafed to a pious man, it opens mostly: *Ma'aseh be-Hasid ehad*, 'there is a story of a Hasid ...' But we may safely say that for the religious consciousness of Judaism as it developed from talmudic times and crystallized in the middle ages, the difference between the two types and their specific characteristics became more and more distinct and significant. Particularly, we have a very large literature on the ethical behaviour and the moral ideals of Judaism, a literature which stretches over almost a thousand years and which was destined not so much for the use of the scholar but appealed in general to the common reader with a moderate or even less than moderate knowledge of things Jewish. It is this literature, in contradistinction to the proper halakhic or talmudist literature, which not everybody had the prerequisites to understand, that was most influential in bringing the message of Judaism to widest circles. It is in such sources, but also in many other documents of Jewish life from those times, that the distinction between the two types becomes crystal-clear. They may still be mentioned together as a kind of formula (such as in the benediction in the *Shmoneh 'Esreh* Prayer, opening: *'Al Hahassidim we-'al Hazaddikim*), but instead of being understood as some kind of synonyms, they are now perceived as two basically distinctive qualities.

The term Zaddik originates in forensic language. A Zaddik is somebody who has been before the courts and has been found 'not guilty'. In this very sober vein the term has entered Jewish ethics. The Zaddik is the Jew who tries to comply with the commandments of the Law. He would be a Zaddik in the eyes of God if, brought before His court it would be found that he has fulfilled his duties at least more than fifty percent. If the scales of the balance swing even slightly to his favour, he is reckoned among the Zaddikim. We mortals, however, do not know how the balances of God's justice will work. In the eyes of his fellow men the Zaddik is he who tries his best to fulfil the Law as far as it is possible to him. For him, all commandments, all duties put upon him by religion are of equal importance, he tries to pay attention to all of them equally without stressing any particular part of them. To accomplish this, no special grace is required. Everybody is called upon to do his duty to the best of his capacity, and everybody is equipped with sufficient strength and innate judgment to try and to succeed. He may not succeed fully, for there are many pitfalls in the way of man. But the *Zaddik* does not lose sight of the goal, he many stumble seven times, but this will not prevent him from going on and dividing his energies between the manifold tasks he is called upon to fulfil. He is the man who puts harmonious order into his life, or at least tries to do so and essentially succeeds. This order is the order of the Torah, an allcomprehensive ideal of harmony in the deeds and activities of men that leaves no room for extravagance. The Zaddik, as the Talmud says, is not expected to be a man of words, he is to be a man of deeds. He may be a great scholar in the sense which I have described before, but even though he may be devoid of intellectual attainments, if he were a simple and unsophisticated man, he still could be a Zaddik. And even if he fulfils his task fully and is as successful in its realisation as could be wished, he is still a Zaddik and nothing else. And this, indeed, in the eyes of Jewish ethics is very much. The Zaddik, let me put it in a sententious way, is the ideal of the *normal* Jew and if he fulfils all that he sets out to do, he is still the embodiment of the normal Jew at his best. This is the main point, stressed by the tradition of our moralist literature.

In the moral sphere, the ideal of the Zaddik contains indeed an element in common with the ideal of the scholar. This is the sobriety of the ideal, the absence of emotionalism. The Just is balanced in his actions, there is something deeply composed and cool-headed about him, however intense the passion to fulfil the divine command that drives him, may be. He does not lose control of himself. And this is of course the reason that righteousness, the quality of the Zaddik, is generally considered in Jewish tradition as something that can be taught, for which you can be educated and trained. The classical manuals of Jewish morals describe such training for the state of Zaddik, none more stringently than the famous treatise *Mesillat Yesharim,* 'The Path of the Upright' by the Italian poet and mystic Moses Hayim Luzzatto (1740), no doubt one of the noblest products of Hebrew literature. The author, who tried to combine the two ideals of the *Talmid Hakham* and the *Zaddik*, sets out to teach the beginner, step by step, how to achieve these goals which are within the rational grasp and within the power of goodwill implanted in all of us and open to systematic development. Or, as five hundred years before him another moralist, Bahya ben Asher, defined it: 'The main principle of the Torah and her fundament consists in the command that man should break his passions and natural drives and subjugate them to the domination of the rational soul. Whoever accomplishes this and makes his intellect the master of his passion and subdues his animal soul, is called a Zaddik'.[3]

This harmonious and judicious function of the Zaddik who tries to dispense justice by his actions is maintained widely and has been greatly stressed by the mystics of Judaism. One of the great Kabbalists said about seven hundred years ago, pursuing the line of thought which I have just indicated: 'For this is the reason why the Zaddikim are called Just Men, because they put everything in the world, both in the inner and outer world, in its rightful place, and nothing oversteps its prescribed limits, and this is why they are called Just Men'.[4]

This definition dominates large spheres of Jewish ethics, especially in the ethics of the Kabbalists and the Hasidim. The Zaddik puts everything in its proper place. This appears to be a very simple sentence. But the simplicity of this definition should not deceive us as to the messianic implication and the utopic power lodged in such a sentence. For in the eyes of Judaism, a world where everything is in its proper place, would be precisely what is meant by a messianic world, a world redeemed. The idea of the Just Man is thus linked with the messianic idea. The Zaddik who puts everything into harmonious order and causes things to dwell together in this world undisturbed and undivided brings about the revelation of God's unity through the harmonious unity of the world. The disorder in the world is at the heart of injustice, the objectionable and reprehensible is connected to disorder. Therefore, the Just Man, for whom the Torah is a law of order and the guide to order, is concerned with putting the world in order and keeping it so. There is a messianic spark in his activities.

III.

In speaking of the Zaddik I have described the ideal of the average Jew, I might even say, the ideal *ba'albayith*, the family man and citizen of the community. He measures his steps, he weighs his actions, he considers the demands made on him, and by doing so and combining his efforts to those of his like, he creates as it were the Jewish community in its highest form. Of course he will be called up to resist temptation, to prove his worth and to overcome great difficulties, but nothing essentially extraordinary is asked of him. The *Hasid*, whom I am going to discuss now, represents indeed a very different type, is in fact at an opposite pole in the world of human values. In the ethical literature of Judaism and generally wherever the terms are used with more or less precision and a sense of discrimination, being a Zaddik means always distinctly less than being a Hasid. Whereas the Zaddik is the ideal embodiment of the norm, the Hasid is the exceptional type of man. He is the radical Jew who, in trying to follow the spiritual call, goes to extremes. The kind of extremism practised by such devotees has changed considerably in the course of time, but its nature has not. The Hasid does not, like the Zaddik, do what is demanded of him, but goes beyond it. He is never content with the middle road, he does not count his steps. He is the enthusiast, whose radicalism and utter emotional commitment are not to be deterred by bourgeois considerations. The self-restraint, characteristic for the behaviour of the Zaddik, is foreign to his nature. Whatever he does, he does in a spirit of spontaneous exuberance and of supererogation, that is to say, far beyond the requirements of duty.

The Hebrew word *Hesed* is not easy to translate. It combines the meanings of charity, loving-kindness and grace. When we are speaking of God's *Hesed*, in contradistinction to his justice and rigour, we indicate the quality of his boundless generosity, the exuberant and spontaneous nature of His benevolence and grace. The usual translation for Hasid 'pious' does not really render its meaning. When the Psalmist says of God that He is a *Hasid* in all his deeds, he does not mean His piety but those qualities which I have just described. And the human *Hasid*, in his own limited sphere, still represents the same basic qualities which he has made the cornerstone of his moral being. He adds to the severity of the prohibitions by prohibiting himself things which even under the Law are permissible, and he adds to the commandments by doing a lot of things which by law he is not required to do. He demands nothing from others, everything from himself. The 'Sayings of the Fathers' in the Mishnah have the famous definition of the four qualities in man: 'He who says: Mine is mine and thine is thine, that is the average man, and some say, it's the quality of Sodom. Mine is thine and thine is mine, that's the ignorant. Mine is thine and thine is thine, that's the Hasid. Thine is mine and mine is mine, that's the wicked.' The

Zaddik follows a law valid for all. I would say he is the Jewish disciple of Kant in ethics. The Hasid follows a law that is valid and binding only for himself. That makes him often an extravagant figure, bound to arouse antagonism and opposition by the very radicalism of his doings. There is something nonconformist and even an element of holy anarchism in his nature. It is true, in his outward behaviour he submits to the established law in all its rigour, but he transcends it by his spiritual fervour. In rabbinical usage, the term *Hasid* never means or implies an attitude of mind alone, it always carries the connotation of the practical application of such an attitude. The old talmudic phrase very significantly puts together the two terms '*Hasidim ve-anshe ma'-aseh*', Hasidim and men of deeds.

This element of radicalism is always present when the great authorities of Judaism speak of the Hasid and of his quality called *Hasidut*. Maimonides explains[5] that a man who gives equal attention to every *Mitsvah* or commandment, is a Zaddik, but a man who singles out one *Mitsvah* in order to exalt it, to go to extremes in its performance and thus leave the middle road, is a *Hasid*. It is clear from all this, that there is a peculiar emotional element in the *Hasid*. The intensity of emotion which he pours into the execution of the special duties he has taken on himself makes him an enthusiast. Over and over again we hear of Hasidim who take one of the 613 commandments and make it a life task. They elaborate it in richest detail. If they are at the same time scholars, they try to work out all its ramifications and combine sophistication with enthusiasm. If they are unlearned – and a famous saying of the Mishnah notwithstanding, a man could be a Hasid quite independent of learning and even innocent of learning – they think out the widest application of the one great *Mitsvah* for which they live. There were among them specialists in chastity or in charity, specialists in walking in the fear of God or in the application of love.

If a man decides to take the path of *Hasidut*, he has to suffer for it. It is even said that he gets a special angel to guide him on the way of suffering, to enable him to stand up to the vicissitudes of his career. There is thus a basic element of selfdenial and asceticism in this figure, and this, in my opinion, explains a phenomenon of great importance in Jewish history. For all the high evaluation of the hasidic type, there is at the same time some noticeable reservation towards him or even a certain distrust. This finds its expression in the fact that throughout a period of at least fifteen hundred years no organisation of Hasidim as a group has been allowed to come into being. This is all the more remarkable as there was no lack of books propagating the Hasidic type as something of the highest value, both among Spanish and Ashkenasic Jews.

One of the most famous works of medieval Hebrew literature is a rather extensive book called The *Sefer Hasidim*, Book of the Hasidim.[6] It was written during the twelfth and thirteenth centuries in Germany and expressed the ideals of a religious movement called The German Hasidim. Here the virtues and qualities forming the true Hasid were extolled: the renunciation of profane pleasure, the conquering of the temptations of ordinary life, the imperviousness to insult and the bearing of shame without flinching, the acting in every respect within the line of strict justice and the like. But even though there was such a tendency to put the highest value on such qualities, the Hasid remains always an exceptional, an unconventional case, a highly individualistic and strange phenomenon in his milieu. No advice is given as to how to organize such people into a common framework, on the contrary, it is taken for granted that every one of them should be active only within the framework of the community of the common people and not striving to build a community of their own. Therefore we find such Hasidim here and there, in large and small places, but it is obvious that the tendency of the rabbinical authority was to integrate them into the general Jewish community and not to encourage separatism.

This is in marked contrast to similar tendencies within Christianity, where parallel tendencies of Christian radicalism have found their expression in the discipline of monastic life where much of what we would call Hasidic behaviour was preached and practised. Judaism has frowned upon such separate organisation of the people of spirit, of a separate class which was expected to enact the demands of religion in everyday life and leaving it to the rest to muddle through as well as they could. There is an essentially sober streak to Judaism, which, for all its intellectual and emotional commitment to its religious tenets and demands, strove to prevent just this stratification of a religious society which we find in medieval Christianity. It tried, instead, to bind together the disparate elements into one community and to allot to each type, be it the Scholar, the Hasid or the Zaddik, an organic function within this framework.

I have said that the Hasidim were single figures. Let me illustrate this from a very authentic source. We have the lists of martyrs slain in many parts of Germany during the persecutions of the 12th and 13th centuries. Many communities used to write down their names for the memory of subsequent generations and they were recited at the *Yiskor* service (in memory of the dead) on high holidays. Many of these lists have been conserved and published by the historians. They mention the names of the men and women concerned and are extremely reticent in conferring honorific titles. They say that somebody was a scholar or a rabbi and there are several men of this type in most communities. But only here and there, used very sparingly and obviously meant as the highest sign of distinction, we find the title *Hasid* or *Hasidah* added to the name of a man or a woman. None of these Hasidim are at the same time characterized as scholars. And this at a time when the ideals of German Hasidism were widely propagated in these communities. [7]

Whether you are a Hasid or not, is basically a matter of gift and character. It is a propensity which you have or have not. If you have it, you can develop it. But you cannot educate everybody to become a Hasid, as in principle you could educate everybody to become a Zaddik. Rabbi Hayim Vital, one of the great Kabbalists of Safed in the sixteenth century, offers the following explanation of the terms which still clearly indicates the superiority of the Hasid. 'He who conscientiously keeps the 613 commands of the Torah, who perfects his rational soul but has not yet made his good propensities part and parcel of his being and still has to fight for them against his evil inclination – such a one is called a perfect Zaddik. But when his good propensities have become an integral part of his own nature and come to him so naturally as to make him keep the Torah in loving joy without having to fight his evil urge, because his body is purified as if the good was his nature since he came out from his mother's womb – such a one is indeed a perfect Hasid'.[8]

Even in that great manual of moral values which I mentioned before, Moses Hayim Luzzatto when starting discussing the Hasid, in contradistinction to the Zaddik, insists that all the advice or analysis he can give cannot help much. The main thing is, according to him, that only those who have been vouchsafed with a gift of divine grace, who have a particular spark in their soul, may strive for the quality of a Hasid. He embarks on polemics against the vulgar and easy use of the term in order to denote what he calls 'practices that are empty or against commonsense or sound judgment, with constant weeping and excessive bowing and strange mortifications of the flesh, such as immersions in ice-cold water or rolling in the snow. But it is not on them that Hasidut rests'.[9] But whatever Luzzatto's own lofty ideal of the Hasid which is largely identical with what we would call a saint, it is clear that he and his contemporaries had a very definite type in mind when speaking of Hasidim and Hasidut. There existed a pattern of common behaviour which characterized the Hasid as a visible and a very pronounced radical in Jewish society, although there may have been quite a number of invisible though no less pronounced radicals. This pattern showed no basic differences in Turkey, Italy, Holland or Poland.

I have tried to delineate three types which together give us a picture of the moral ideal of Judaism. In the course of history all kind of combinations and alterations have made their appearance. Especially as to the popular usage of Zaddik and Hasid in an unprecise way many examples could be adduced. But surely, no stranger example could be found than the metamorphosis of the terms in the Hasidic movement of the 18th century originating in Podolia and Volhynia and centred around the figure of Israel Ba'al Shem Tov who died in 1760. It is in many ways a striking illustration for some of the points I have made here, particularly regarding the organization of the people of Hasidic type. For only as an organization where all kind of people gathered around a central figure which was of truly Hasidic type, could Hasidism maintain itself.

If the leaders would have stuck together and formed a body composed exclusively of people of their own type, the movement would have succumbed under the onslaught of old-fashioned rabbinical Judaism whose antagonism it could not fail to arouse anyway. We would not be talking of a specific world of Hasidism, in the sense of the word as it is used with regard to this movement, some of whose ramifications are still with us, were it not for its success in placing the figure of the Jewish saint as a radical Jew into an organic Jewish social body.

A very curious metamorphosis of terms has, however, taken place here. Never would it have occurred to earlier generations, neither in literature nor in life, to give the title of *Hasidim* to people who admired Hasidim. But this is precisely what has happened here. People who admired the living embodiments of Hasidic ideals, called themselves Hasidim, – a rather paradoxical, if not to say scandalous usage of the word – and the true Hasidim, those who live up to the ideal, came now to be called Zaddikim. This novel turn of the terminology is surely highly confusing. A Zaddik in the Hasidic sense has nothing to do with what the term meant in the traditional usage which I have tried to explain, but rather connotes the 'Super-Hasid'. It is beyond the scope of this lecture to explain the historical reasons for this change and the processes by which it came about. What we are concerned with is the understanding of the essential meaning of the three types, of the phenomena themselves, by whatever name they may be known.

Let me close with a remark about a figure of Jewish popular tradition in which the original figure of the Hasid has reached a climax. This is the concept of the so-called hidden or *concealed Zaddikim* which since the time of the Hasidic movement has held a place of honour in Jewish legend. Its roots are very old. The famous teacher Rabbi Shimon ben Yohai in the 2nd century was credited with the saying: 'The world never lacks thirty Zaddikim like Abraham'. They protect the world, just as Abraham did in his own time. Later on, another Talmudic teacher maintained that in every generation the world has no fewer than thirty-six just men, who are vouchsafed the vision of the countenance of God. This is the source of the concept of the thirty-six hidden Zaddikim of the popular legend, called in Yiddish *Lamedvov-niks*, according to the Hebrew denotation of the number thirty-six. It is on them and their merit that the world rests.[10]

There were two types of Zaddikim, those who are hidden and keep to themselves and those who manifest themselves to their fellow-men and are working as it were under the public eye. The former is called a *Nistar*, i. e. a concealed one, and the latter *Mephursam*, i. e. famous. The hidden Zaddikim are of the higher order, because they are not tempted by the vanity almost inseparable from a public career.[11] Indeed, some of them take it upon themselves to build up an image in sharp contradiction to their true and hidden nature. They may not even be aware of their own nature and go about performing their good deeds in secret without knowing that they are of the elect. They are hidden not only from mankind but from themselves. Eastern Jewish folklore was indefatigable in elaborating these aspects and particularly their paradoxical side. Legend has it that one of the thirty-six is the Messiah and would reveal himself as such, if only his generation were worthy of redemption. You can never know who these highest bearers of moral standards are. One of them, and this is the final moral, to which this idea points, may be your neighbour.

NOTES

1. *b. Baba bathra* 8a.
2. *b. Menahoth* 29a.
3. *Kad ha-Kemah*, ed. Ch. Breit, vol. II, Bl. 10a.
4. J. Gikatilla, *Scha'arei Zedek*, 1785, Bl. 16a.
5. Maimonides in his commentary on the *Mishnah*, tr. *Avot V* § 7.
6. Cf. my *Major Trends in Jewish Mysticism*. Ch. 3, pp. 91–99.
7. This holds true even for later periods. Isaac Markon has remarked (in his article in the last volume, 79, of the Monatsschrift für Geschichte und Wissenschaft des Judentums, 1939, published without pagination) how restrained the usage of the term *Hasid* still was between 1650–1750.
8. Vital, *Sha'arei Kedusha* I, § 3. His source was Maimonides, *Shmona PeraKim*, Ch. 6.
9. *Mesillath Yesharim*, Ch. 18.
10. Cf. my essay on this concept of the Hidden Zaddikim in *Judaica* I, 1963, pp. 216–225.
11. This is stated by Benjamin of Zalozitz, *Torei Zahav*, 1816, f. 34b, and *Amtachat Benjamin* f. 78c.